THE ULTIMATE

10

Entertainment

MOVIE CHARACTERS

By Mark Stewart

Gareth Stevens
Publishing

Please visit our web site at **www.garethstevens.com.**
For a free catalog describing Gareth Stevens Publishing's list of high-quality books, call 1-800-542-2595 (USA) or 1-800-387-3178 (Canada). Gareth Stevens Publishing's fax: 1-877-542-2596

Library of Congress Cataloging-in-Publication Data
Stewart, Mark, 1960–
   Movie characters / by Mark Stewart.
       p. cm. — (Ultimate 10: entertainment)
   Includes bibliographical references and index.
   ISBN-10: 0-8368-9164-3   ISBN-13: 978-0-8368-9164-5 (lib. bdg.)
   ISBN-10: 1-4339-2212-6   ISBN-13: 978-1-4339-2212-1 (softcover)
   1. Characters and characteristics in motion pictures—Juvenile literature. I. Title.
PN1995.9.C36S73 2009
791.43'652—dc22   2009010534

This edition first published in 2010 by
Gareth Stevens Publishing
A Weekly Reader® Company
1 Reader's Digest Road
Pleasantville, NY 10570-7000 USA

Copyright © 2010 by Gareth Stevens, Inc.

Executive Managing Editor: Lisa M. Herrington
Senior Designer: Keith Plechaty

Produced by Editorial Directions, Inc.
Art Direction and Page Production: The Design Lab

Picture credits
Key: c = center, b = bottom, l = left, r = right, t = top
Cover, title page: (background) Shutterstock, (c) Shutterstock, (c) ©Warner Brothers/courtesy Everett Collection, (bl) ©Everett Collection; p. 3: Shutterstock; p. 4-5: ©DreamWorks/courtesy Everett Collection; p. 5: (r) Shutterstock; p. 6: (t) Shutterstock, (b) Shutterstock; p. 7, ©Everett Collection; p. 8: (t) ©Everett Collection, (b) Virgil Apger/John Kobal Foundation/Getty Images; p. 9: (t) Michael Ochs Archive/Getty Images, (b) Shutterstock; p. 10: (t) Shutterstock, (b) Shutterstock; p. 11: (t) ©Paramount Pictures/courtesy Everett Collection, (b) Shutterstock; p. 12: (t) ©Paramount Pictures/courtesy Everett Collection, (b) ©Paramount Pictures/courtesy Everett Collection; p. 13: (t) ©Paramount Pictures/courtesy Everett Collection, (b) Shutterstock; p. 14: (t) Shutterstock, (b) Shutterstock; p. 15: ©Chip East/Reuters/Corbis; p. 16: (t) ©Photos 12/Alamy, (b) © Photos 12/Alamy p. 17: (t) ©Photos 12/Alamy, (b) Shutterstock; p. 18: (t) Shutterstock, (b) Shutterstock; p. 19: ©Everett Collection; p. 20: ©Everett Collection; p. 21: (c) ©Warner Brothers/courtesy Everett Collection, (b) Shutterstock; p. 22: (t) Shutterstock, (b) Shutterstock; p. 23: ©Warner Brothers/courtesy Everett Collection; p. 24: (t) ©Warner Brothers/courtesy Everett Collection, (b) ©Warner Brothers/courtesy Everett Collection; p. 25: (t) ©Warner Bothers/courtesy Everett Collection, (b) Shutterstock; p. 26: (t) Shutterstock, (b) Shutterstock; p. 27: ©Everett Collection; p. 28: ©Everett Collection; p. 29: (t) Shutterstock, (b) ©MGM/courtesy Everett Collection; p. 30: (t) Shutterstock, (b) Shutterstock; p. 31: ©Walt Disney/courtesy Everett Collection; p. 32: (t) ©Walt Disney/courtesy Everett Collection, (b) ©Buena Vista Pictures/courtesy Everett Collection; p. 33: (t) ©Walt Disney/courtesy Everett Collection, (b) Shutterstock; p. 34: (t) Shutterstock, (b) Shutterstock; p. 35: ©Paramount/courtesy Everett Collection; p. 36: ©DreamWorks/courtesy Everett Collection; p. 37: (t) Shutterstock, (b) ©Paramount/courtesy Everett Collection; p. 38: (t) Shutterstock, (b) Shutterstock; p. 39: ©Columbia/courtesy Everett Collection; p. 40: ©Columbia/courtesy Everett Collection; p. 41: (t) ©Sony Pictures/courtesy Everett Collection, (b) Shutterstock; p. 42: (t) Shutterstock, (b) Shutterstock; p. 43: ©Everett Collection; p. 44: ©Paramount/courtesy Everett Collection; p. 45: (c) ©Paramount/courtesy Everett Collection, (b) Shutterstock; p. 46: (t) ©Fox Searchlight/courtesy Everett Collection, (b) ©Everett Collection

Printed in the United States of America

1 2 3 4 5 6 7 8 9 14 13 12 11 10 09

TABLE OF CONTENTS

Words in the glossary appear in **bold** type
the first time they are used in the text

THE ULTIMATE 10

Entertainment

MOVIE CHARACTERS

Welcome to The Ultimate 10! This exciting series highlights the very best from the world of entertainment.

When an actor agrees to play a part in a movie, no one can be certain of the result. Sometimes, the character is good but the movie is not. Sometimes, it's the other way around. Every so often, a special actor plays a part in a way that makes both the character and the film unforgettable.

Shrek, an ogre with a heart of gold, falls in love with Princess Fiona in the movie *Shrek*.

This book tells the stories of 10 "ultimate" movie characters. In many cases, they have become more famous than the movies themselves. In fact, you may know about them already—even though you haven't seen their movies!

Learn about the people playing these remarkable roles. Discover why the characters are legendary. Once you recognize the things that make a character great, you may never watch a movie the same way again.

Classic Characters

Here are 10 heroes, villains, and friends that movie lovers will never forget:

#1 Dorothy Gale

#2 Forrest Gump

#3 Darth Vader

#4 Harry Potter

#5 The Joker

#6 James Bond

#7 Jack Sparrow

#8 Shrek

#9 Spider-Man

#10 Indiana Jones

#1

Dorothy Gale
There's No Place Like Home

"There's no place like home." Dorothy Gale repeats that famous phrase three times after tapping the heels of her ruby red slippers three times. By the end of the 1939 movie, the star of *The Wizard of Oz* had tapped her way into the hearts of movie audiences. She also became one of the most memorable characters in film history. Although Dorothy began as a book character, it was actress Judy Garland who brought the Kansas farm girl to life.

CHARACTER STUDY

Character: Dorothy Gale
Creator: L. Frank Baum
Movie: *The Wizard of Oz*
Year: 1939
Actress: Judy Garland

Book Smart

Children's author L. Frank Baum created Dorothy. She first appeared in his 1900 book *The Wonderful Wizard of Oz*. Baum was greatly influenced by *Alice in Wonderland*. In both books, a young girl enters a strange dream world. There, she meets twisted versions of people she knows in real life.

Finding an actress to play Dorothy for the 1939 film was not easy. She had to be a good actress and be able to sing emotional songs like "Over the Rainbow." Many people thought that Shirley Temple should play the part. Temple was the top child actor of the 1930s. Her singing style was not quite right, though. The final choice was Judy Garland. She turned out to be perfect for the part.

CLASSIC QUOTE

"I'm not a witch at all. I'm Dorothy Gale from Kansas."

—Dorothy, explaining herself to Glinda, the Good Witch of the North

Judy Garland was only 16 when she got the part of Dorothy.

American Icon

The lessons Dorothy learns during her adventure in Oz sent a message to audiences in the 1930s. During the **Great Depression**, many young people left rural areas to seek work in cities. The magic words "There's no place like home" encouraged people to stay with their families, work hard, and hope for better days.

Dorothy sings "Over the Rainbow" on her Kansas farm while imagining brighter worlds. She soon wakes up in Oz.

Dorothy was a beloved children's book character before *The Wizard of Oz* was made. The movie turned Dorothy into an American **icon**. Generations of young girls have idolized her. Kids love dressing as Dorothy—with her pigtails and checked dress—for Halloween.

SUPER SIDEKICKS

Dorothy is not the only character in *The Wizard of Oz* to become a legend. Here are some of the movie's other classic characters and the actors who played them:

Character	Actor
Scarecrow	Ray Bolger
Tin Man	Jack Haley
Cowardly Lion	Bert Lahr
Wicked Witch of the West	Margaret Hamilton

The Spirit of Dorothy

The character Dorothy appeared in many later films. She did not look the way Judy Garland did, but her spirit remained the same. An animated film called *Journey Back to Oz* was made in the 1960s. Garland's daughter Liza Minnelli was the voice of Dorothy. In *The Wiz* (1978), Dorothy is a shy city schoolteacher leaving her neighborhood for the first time. In 1985, Dorothy is the star of a **sequel** called *Return to Oz*. In the sequel, Dorothy is asked to save the Emerald City.

Diana Ross starred as Dorothy in the 1978 film *The Wiz*. Michael Jackson (far left) played the Scarecrow.

DID YOU KNOW?

L. Frank Baum chose the name Dorothy Gale in honor of his niece Dorothy Gage. Dorothy Gage had died when she was just a baby.

2

Forrest Gump
Witness to History

Filmmakers sometimes use the adventures of one character to explore history. In 1994, director Robert Zemeckis showed how the culture of the United States had changed. He did it through the character Forrest Gump. At first, this seemed like an odd choice. Forrest is not very smart. He is slow to react to events around him. Yet the world seen through Forrest's eyes is revealing. Audiences saw the turbulent 1960s and 1970s simply and truthfully—just as Forrest did.

CHARACTER STUDY

Character: Forrest Gump
Creator: Winston Groom
Movie: *Forrest Gump*
Year: 1994
Actors: Tom Hanks (Forrest as an adult) and Michael Conner Humphreys (Forrest as a child)

In the movie, Forrest Gump tells the story of his life while sitting on a park bench.

Groomed for Greatness

Forrest was the creation of writer Winston Groom. His book *Forrest Gump* was published in 1986. In the book, Forrest has many of the same experiences as the movie character. He also has many adventures that didn't make it into the film. In the book, he is captured by cannibals, and he goes into outer space.

Several actors were offered the part before Tom Hanks agreed to play Forrest. Chevy Chase, John Travolta, and Bill Murray all turned it down. Forrest was a difficult character to play, but Hanks made him real. *Forrest Gump* won six **Academy Awards**, including best picture and best actor.

CLASSIC QUOTE

"Mama always said life was like a box of chocolates. You never know what you're gonna get."
—Forrest Gump

Forrest (left) often finds himself in the middle of historic events. Here, he attends an antiwar rally in Washington, D.C.

Touching Performance

Critics and movie fans loved Forrest. Hanks played him like a big, lovable kid. Forrest is generous and loyal. He can be funny and heartbreaking at the same time. In that way, he truly reflects the world around him. He lives through the Vietnam War, antiwar protests, and rapid changes of the 1960s and 1970s.

HERE AND NOW

Early in the movie, young Forrest meets future music legend Elvis Presley. The filmmakers used computer animation to place Forrest next to other historical figures. Here are some of his famous "costars" from the movie:

Historical Figure	Position
John F. Kennedy	U.S. president
Lyndon B. Johnson	U.S. president
Richard M. Nixon	U.S. president
John Lennon	Singer

Forrest shares the screen with President Kennedy.

Smart Move

In most movies, the main character changes and grows. The charm of Forrest Gump is that he stays the same while the world changes around him. Forrest may not understand everything, but he gets to the heart of the matter. He tells Jenny, his childhood friend whom he grows to love, "I may not be a smart man, but I know what love is." During the movie, the other characters come to appreciate how "smart" Forrest really is.

During the movie, Forrest runs across the entire United States. "Run, Forrest, Run" became a popular phrase from the film.

DID YOU KNOW?

The filmmakers did not only use computer animation to add people and scenery to *Forrest Gump*. The same technology was used to "remove" the legs of actor Gary Sinise. Sinise played Lieutenant Dan, who loses his legs in the Vietnam War.

#3

Darth Vader
Welcome to the Dark Side

Not every great movie character is a hero. Audiences love—and fear—a great villain just as much. That explains the popularity of Darth Vader from the first three *Star Wars* films. What could make someone so hate-filled that he could destroy whole planets? In later *Star Wars* films, fans saw the cruel twists of fate that led Darth Vader to the dark side.

CHARACTER STUDY

Character: Darth Vader
Creator: George Lucas
Movie: *Star Wars*
Year: 1977
Actors: David Prowse and James Earl Jones

PRODUCTION
DIRECTOR
CAMERA
DATE   SCENE   TAKE

Super-Sized Evil

When George Lucas started dreaming up characters for *Star Wars*, he needed a great bad guy for his heroes to fight. He wanted a larger-than-life villain who was half man and half machine. Darth Vader's costume was influenced by Lucas's love of **samurai** warriors from Japanese history.

David Prowse played Darth Vader in the first three *Star Wars* films. Prowse stands 6 feet 7 inches (201 centimenters) tall. The British actor had played other towering characters, such as Frankenstein. He was given a choice: He could play Darth Vader or he could play Chewbacca, the giant, furry copilot of a spaceship. Prowse wanted to play the villain.

However, Lucas knew that Prowse's voice was not scary enough for the role. He selected James Earl Jones to provide Vader's deep, powerful voice. To create Vader's famous heavy breathing, a **sound designer** recorded himself breathing with scuba gear.

CLASSIC QUOTE
"Don't underestimate the Force."
—Darth Vader

Two actors and clever sound effects brought Darth Vader to life.

Trick or Treat!

The first *Star Wars* movie was a smash hit. Afterward, Lucas's company began "merchandising" the characters—making toys, books, action figures, and other products for kids. Darth Vader items were just as popular as those that showed the film's heroes.

Fans also showed just how much they loved Darth Vader at Halloween. Darth Vader costumes were among the hottest sellers 30 years ago. They still are today.

Luke Skywalker battles Darth Vader in *The Empire Strikes Back.*

❝ *Darth* is a variation of dark. And *Vader* is a variation of father. So it's basically Dark Father. ❞
—Director George Lucas to *Rolling Stone* magazine on where he got Darth Vader's name

BAD DUDES

Darth Vader was just one of the unforgettable bad guys in the *Star Wars* films. Here are some of the others:

Villain	Actor
Jabba the Hutt	Larry Ward (voice)
General Grievous	Matthew Wood (voice)
Count Dooku	Christopher Lee
Darth Maul (right)	Ray Park, Peter Serafinowicz (voice)
Palpatine/Darth Sidious	Ian McDiarmid

Good and Evil

In the 1977 film, the hero, Luke Skywalker, represents good. Darth Vader represents evil. With each new *Star Wars* film, it became clearer to fans that things were not so black and white. The last three films focused on how Anakin Skywalker turned to the dark side and became Darth Vader. After six films released over nearly 30 years, audiences realized that Vader was the story's main character.

Hayden Christensen stars as young Anakin Skywalker.

DID YOU KNOW?

In the *Star Wars* films, fans got to see Darth Vader as a young boy and as an old man. In *The Phantom Menace*, Jake Lloyd plays nine-year-old Anakin Skywalker. Sebastian Shaw was the face that fans saw when the dying Vader was unmasked near the end of *Return of the Jedi*.

#4

Harry Potter
Boy Wizard

When author J. K. Rowling began writing the Harry Potter novels, she did not imagine Harry as a movie character. He belonged to the dark, dreamlike world of wizards. Countless young fans grew up with Harry. When Harry hit the screen, they could grow up with him all over again. This time, however, they could see the people and places they had only imagined before.

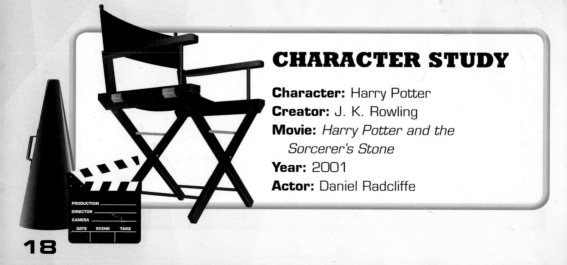

CHARACTER STUDY

Character: Harry Potter
Creator: J. K. Rowling
Movie: *Harry Potter and the Sorcerer's Stone*
Year: 2001
Actor: Daniel Radcliffe

PRODUCTION
DIRECTOR
CAMERA
DATE   SCENE   TAKE

Finding Harry

J. K. Rowling used her imagination to go "from rags to riches." She got her idea for a book about a young wizard during a long train ride. She was almost penniless when she finished the first Harry Potter novel, in 1995. It was published in 1997 and became a best seller. In 1998, Warner Bros. bought the **rights** to make her book into a movie.

Rowling insisted that the film be shot in England, with English actors. The search for the perfect Harry began. Daniel Radcliffe was discovered while acting in a play called *Stones in His Pockets*. He was 11 years old. Rowling saw Radcliffe's **screen test** and said she didn't think it was possible to find "a better Harry."

CLASSIC QUOTE

"I don't go looking for trouble. Trouble usually finds me."
—Harry Potter

Eleven-year-old Daniel Radcliffe was the perfect Harry Potter.

Perfectly Harry

Every so often, the world falls in love with a young actor. From the moment Daniel Radcliffe first appeared on the screen as Harry, audiences adored him. Radcliffe *was* Harry Potter! He looked just like the Harry they knew from the book cover. Harry has his father's messy black hair and his mother's green eyes. He also bears the scar from his first meeting with Lord Voldemort, his enemy.

Harry's pet owl, Hedwig, helps him on many of his adventures.

SCHOOL YEARS

Each movie in the Harry Potter series covers one year at the Hogwarts School of Witchcraft and Wizardry:

Movie	Harry's Age	Year
Harry Potter and the Sorcerer's Stone	11	2001
Harry Potter and the Chamber of Secrets	12	2002
Harry Potter and the Prisoner of Azkaban	13	2004
Harry Potter and the Goblet of Fire	14	2005
Harry Potter and the Order of the Phoenix	15	2007
Harry Potter and the Half-Blood Prince	16	2009
Harry Potter and the Deathly Hallows	17	*

*The final book will be made into two movies.

Growing Up

With each new movie, Harry Potter grows up a little more and faces greater challenges. He starts out as a shy, innocent boy and slowly becomes a complex young man. His relationships with his best friends, Ron and Hermione, change and grow stronger. The three friends learn that courage and friendship are their greatest possessions.

Harry's battles with Lord Voldemort kept fans on the edge of their seats. Would good triumph over evil? They could hardly wait for Rowling to finish her last book. They want to see it for themselves in the movies, too!

Hermione, Ron, and Harry face a werewolf in *Harry Potter and the Prisoner of Azkaban*.

DID YOU KNOW?

Three actors besides Daniel Radcliffe have portrayed Harry Potter. Triplets named Saunders were used when the script called for a scene with Harry as a baby.

#5

The Joker
Crazy Bad

Every great superhero needs a great villain. Through the decades, Batman has battled many evil foes. The greatest of them is the Joker. Many actors have played the Joker. Each brought something new to the role. In *The Dark Knight*, Heath Ledger put his own spin on the character. He played the Joker as a madman—and breathed new life into a classic bad guy.

CHARACTER STUDY

Character: The Joker
Creators: Jerry Robinson, Bill Finger, and Bob Kane
Movie: *The Dark Knight*
Year: 2008
Actor: Heath Ledger

PRODUCTION
DIRECTOR
CAMERA
DATE   SCENE   TAKE

In *The Dark Knight*, the Joker's dirty green hair and messy face paint give him a terrifying appearance.

Familiar Foe

The Joker is Batman's oldest enemy. He appeared in the first issue of the *Batman* comic book, in 1940. The Joker's bleached-white skin and wild grin were inspired by a movie character. The character is from a 1928 film called *The Man Who Laughs*.

The first actor to play the Joker on screen was Cesar Romero. He starred in the 1960s *Batman* TV show and the 1966 *Batman* movie. Romero played the Joker as a mostly comic character. Jack Nicholson starred as the Joker in the blockbuster 1989 *Batman* movie. Critics raved about his performance. Although his Joker was funny, he was also a killer.

Director Christopher Nolan wanted Heath Ledger to play the Joker in *The Dark Knight*. They agreed that he should be crazier and more evil than any movie villain in history. Other actors wanted the part, including Robin Williams, Adrien Brody, and Steve Carell, but Nolan stuck with Ledger.

CLASSIC QUOTE

"I won't kill you because you're just too much fun. I think you and I are destined to do this forever."

—Heath Ledger as the Joker, speaking to Batman

No Laughing Matter

Heath Ledger's Joker left audiences spellbound. He looked like an insane clown. His costume and makeup were terrifying. Ledger's Joker is more clever and unpredictable than ever. He pushes Batman to the limit of his abilities.

In *The Dark Knight*, the Joker isn't driven by greed, like other criminals. In one scene, he burns a huge pyramid of money.

Sadly, Ledger died before the movie was released. The news of his death added to talk about his amazing performance as the Joker. Everyone wanted to see *The Dark Knight*. By early 2009, the movie had made more than $1 billion around the world. Ledger won an Academy Award for best supporting actor for his performance.

CRIMINAL MINDS

The Joker isn't the only villain who Batman has battled in the movies. Here are some of best, and the actors who played them:

Villain	Actor
The Penguin	Danny DeVito (right), Burgess Meredith
The Riddler	Jim Carrey, Frank Gorshin
Catwoman	Michelle Pfeiffer, Lee Meriwether
Mr. Freeze	Arnold Schwarzenegger
Two-Face	Aaron Eckhart, Tommy Lee Jones
Scarecrow	Cillian Murphy

ISO 64

26

Jack Nicholson starred as the Joker in the 1989 *Batman* movie.

Real Bad

Since the Joker first battled Batman in the comics, he has become less of a cartoon character. Now, he is more like a real person. He kills with knives, guns, and explosives—not with tricks like poison-squirting flowers. When the Joker was just a colorful "bad guy" he didn't seem real. Now, he is scarier than ever. He is a character that no one can forget.

DID YOU KNOW?

In the comic, the Joker got his strange skin and hair after falling into a vat of chemicals. In *The Dark Knight*, audiences aren't told why he looks the way he does. They have to guess.

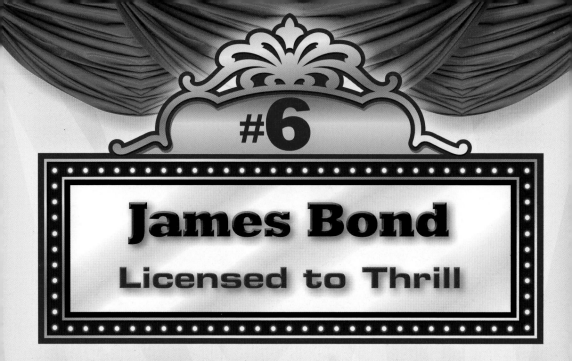

#6

James Bond
Licensed to Thrill

No character on the big screen delivers more thrills, chills, action, and romance than James Bond. Bond is a secret agent code-named 007. In a long string of action-packed movies, he has stopped the evil plans of madmen on land, under the sea, and even in outer space. He is smart, strong, and cool-headed. With the help of some fantastic gadgets, Bond has become the coolest action hero in movie history.

CHARACTER STUDY

Character: James Bond
Creator: Ian Fleming
Movie: *Dr. No*
Year: 1963
Actor: Sean Connery

PRODUCTION
DIRECTOR
CAMERA
DATE   SCENE   TAKE

Sean Connery, as James Bond, leans on his Aston Martin in *Goldfinger*. Bond's sports cars often have cool gadgets that help him escape from danger.

The Birth of Bond

Writer Ian Fleming dreamed up Agent 007 in the 1950s. In Fleming's secret world of spies, the best agents are called 00 agents. That means they are licensed to kill. Fleming wrote 14 James Bond books and nine short stories between 1953 and 1964. The first one to be turned into a movie was *Dr. No*.

To make the film a hit, the perfect actor was needed. When director Terence Young chose 6-foot 2-inch (188-cm) Sean Connery, Fleming was unhappy. He called Connery an "overgrown stunt man." He thought Connery was too rough and too physical to play the sophisticated Bond character.

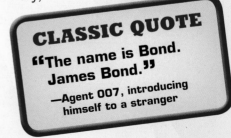

CLASSIC QUOTE

"The name is Bond. James Bond."

—Agent 007, introducing himself to a stranger

Movie Makeover

Dr. No was a huge hit. As Bond, Sean Connery was graceful and worldly. Terence Young had given Connery lessons on behaving like a gentleman. In the process, Young totally transformed him! Connery's Bond was also tough and fearless enough to take on any villain.

The biggest thumbs-up came from Ian Fleming himself. He was so impressed by Connery that he changed the remaining Bond books to give his hero a Scottish background much like Connery's.

Sean Connery searches for a missing agent in the 1962 Bond film *Dr. No*.

"I wanted the simplest, dullest, plainest-sounding name I could find."
—Ian Fleming, on why he named his hero James Bond

CALLING ALL AGENTS

Many actors have played James Bond, on radio, on TV, and in the movies. These six are the only "official" ones:

Actor	# of Bond Movies	Years
Sean Connery	7	1962–1967, 1971, 1983
George Lazenby	1	1969
Roger Moore	7	1973–1985
Timothy Dalton	2	1987–1989
Pierce Brosnan	4	1995–2004
Daniel Craig	2	2006–present

One of the funniest big-screen characters in history is Austin Powers, played by Mike Myers. The Austin Powers movies were inspired by the James Bond series. Many of the characters in the Powers movies are funny versions of characters in the Bond films.

Super Spy

After more than 40 years and 20 films, James Bond remains the number-one movie spy. Bond films have made more than $4 billion worldwide. Every so often, a new actor brings something different to the role.

In 2006, Daniel Craig became the sixth actor to play Agent 007. In *Casino Royale* and *Quantum of Solace*, he played Bond as a cool and violent secret agent. Fans of Fleming's books loved his performance. They said that Craig was the first film Bond that was true to the original.

Daniel Craig starred as Bond in the 2008 film *Quantum of Solace*.

7

Jack Sparrow
The Perfect Pirate

Over the years, countless actors have played pirates in movies. But movie fans had never seen a pirate quite like Jack Sparrow before. He looks death in the eye but runs from danger. Was he a scoundrel or a hero? A gentleman or a villain? Audiences did not know what to think. One thing was certain, however: Johnny Depp had created one of the most unique characters of all time.

CHARACTER STUDY

Character: Captain Jack Sparrow
Creators: Ted Elliott and Terry Rossio
Movie: *Pirates of the Caribbean: The Curse of the Black Pearl*
Year: 2003
Actor: Johnny Depp

Something Special

The Pirates of the Caribbean is a popular ride at Disney theme parks. When Walt Disney Studios decided to turn the ride into a movie, the studio knew it was taking a risk. Pirate movies were rarely successful. Plus, no one had ever based a movie on a ride before. At first, the writers wanted to focus on the story of a handsome young blacksmith named Will Turner and a lovely woman named Elizabeth Swann. Elizabeth is kidnapped by pirates, and Will tries to rescue her.

Johnny Depp was cast as the third leading character, Jack Sparrow. Depp played the pirate captain in a much different way than filmmakers expected. He slurred his speech and made wild gestures. No one was sure how audiences would react to his performance.

> ### CLASSIC QUOTE
> **"I admire a person who's willing to do whatever's necessary."**
> —Jack Sparrow, to Elizabeth Swann

Johnny Depp helped develop Jack Sparrow's look. The character has long hair and wears a leather hat.

Stealing the Show

Pirates of the Caribbean: The Curse of the Black Pearl was the hit of the summer in 2003. It had sword-fighting, romance, and amazing special effects. Still, Depp stole the show as Jack Sparrow. In the role, Depp was

Jack Sparrow and Will Turner (played by Orlando Bloom) face off in *The Curse of the Black Pearl.*

funny but he also proved himself to be a great action star. Sparrow uses his charm to get what he wants. His character uses his wits to escape from impossible situations. He will stop at nothing to recover his ship, *The Black Pearl.* Moviegoers weren't sure whether Sparrow was a hero or villain until the end of the movie.

ROCK AND ROLL PIRATE

Johnny Depp researched pirates of the 1700s as preparation for playing Jack Sparrow. He decided that pirates were the rock stars of the time. Depp modeled Jack Sparrow on rock star Keith Richards of the Rolling Stones. He has the same long hair and wild image. In the third *Pirates of the Caribbean* movie, Richards (right) was cast as Sparrow's father!

Audiences love Jack Sparrow's outrageous appearance and personality.

A Good Guy

Depp's performance helped the film make more than $650 million worldwide. Two more *Pirates of the Caribbean* films were quickly scheduled. *Dead Man's Chest* came out in 2006, and *At World's End* followed in 2007. In those films, Jack Sparrow's fans got a better idea of what makes him tick. Despite Sparrow's trickery and lies, he is loyal to his friends. Perhaps a pirate can be a good guy, after all.

DID YOU KNOW?

Jack Sparrow became so popular that Disney added an **animatronic** version of Sparrow to the Pirates of the Caribbean ride.

#8

Shrek
Ogre Time

Classic movie heroes have good looks and a terrific personality. So how did Shrek become a star? The animated ogre is rude, crude, smelly, and … green. He lives in a world where fairy tales are turned upside down. In this place, Shrek turns out to be the perfect leading man! The movie's message made Shrek an unforgettable figure. The message? If you are comfortable in your own skin, others will see the real you. Even if you're green.

CHARACTER STUDY

Character: Shrek
Creator: William Steig
Movie: *Shrek*
Year: 2001
Actor: Mike Myers

PRODUCTION
DIRECTOR
CAMERA
DATE   SCENE   TAKE

Mike to the Rescue

William Steig dreamed up Shrek. Steig was a popular cartoonist and children's book author. In 1990, at the age of 83, Steig published a picture book called *Shrek!* Steig agreed to let DreamWorks Pictures make a movie of his book.

The animation for *Shrek* was completed in 2000. Comedian Chris Farley started recording the lovable monster's voice. Halfway through, Farley died suddenly. Mike Myers was brought in to rerecord the **dialogue**. When Myers saw a rough version of the film, he asked to redo Shrek's voice. He thought the character would sound better with a Scottish accent.

Mike Myers was a perfect fit for Shrek.

CLASSIC QUOTE

"Ogres are like onions. ... Onions have layers. Ogres have layers."

—Shrek

On his quest to rescue the beautiful Princess Fiona, Shrek finds that he has fallen in love with her.

Smash Hit

Shrek was a smash hit. Kids loved the movie. Grown-ups loved the movie. It was filled with hilarious fairy-tale jokes. Some of the best lines were delivered by Shrek's friend Donkey. He became one of the great **sidekicks** in movie history. Myers's last-minute accent change was a perfect touch. The Scottish accent he used for Shrek gave the ogre a touch of class.

I KNOW THAT VOICE!

Some of the top names in Hollywood lent their talents to *Shrek*.

Character	Actor
Shrek	Mike Myers
Donkey	Eddie Murphy
Fiona	Cameron Diaz
Lord Farquaad	John Lithgow

DID YOU KNOW?

The actors playing the main characters in *Shrek* never worked together. They recorded their parts separately.

Learning Experience

In his first movie, Shrek falls in love and gains confidence in himself. In *Shrek 2*, he learns how to be part of a family. He must struggle to keep his family together. In *Shrek the Third*, the lovable ogre discovers the pressures that come with greater responsibility. He uses this lesson to become a smart leader and a great dad.

> **"I think Shrek is a classic, a fairy tale classic."**
> —Mike Myers

In *Shrek the Third*, Shrek must bring Fiona's cousin Artie back to the land of Far Far Away to become the new king.

#9

Spider-Man
Web Slinger

Moviemakers face big challenges when they turn a comic book superhero into a movie superhero. The movie has to satisfy fans who have been reading the comic books for decades. It has to include special effects that give the hero superpowers. The makers of *Spider-Man* also had to find an actor who could make the character both human and heroic. Tobey Maguire did just that. He made Peter Parker awkward, Spider-Man unstoppable, and the character unforgettable.

CHARACTER STUDY

Character: Spider-Man
Creators: Stan Lee and Steve Ditko
Movie: *Spider-Man*
Year: 2002
Actor: Tobey Maguire

Special effects helped bring Spidey's web-slinging adventures to the big screen.

Teen Sensation

Spider-Man began life in 1962 as a Marvel Comics superhero. Stan Lee came up with the character while watching a fly on a wall. Lee got the idea for a superhero who could crawl up walls. Spider-Man was born.

Lee wanted kids to be able to relate to the character. Peter Parker has superpowers, but he has the same problems as other teenagers. *Spider-Man* was a hit, especially with teen readers.

In the late 1970s, fans began asking for a Spider-Man movie. It took nearly 25 years for the right script, the right actors, and the right special effects to come together. Finally, in 2002, *Spider-Man* reached the big screen.

CLASSIC QUOTE
"[I'm] your friendly neighborhood Spider-Man."
—Spider-Man

True to the Comics

Spider-Man battles the Green Goblin in the first film.

Director Sam Raimi wanted to stay close to the comic book character. He did not want to disappoint fans of "Spidey." Tobey Maguire was the perfect choice to play the lead role. He was believable as the awkward teenager Peter Parker. He also held his own in the action sequences as Spider-Man. For Spidey's breathtaking web-swinging stunts, Raimi used amazing **computer-generated imagery (CGI).** The final result was spectacular. The movie made more than $100 million its first weekend. Earnings reached $400 million by the time the film left theaters.

MORTAL ENEMIES

Some great villains come to life in the *Spider-Man* movies. In the first film, Spider-Man faces Norman Osborn. After testing a strength enhancer, he becomes the superpowerful Green Goblin. In *Spider-Man 2*, Spidey battles Dr. Otto Octavius. He is a scientist whose experiments go bad. After he gets four mechanical arms, he becomes Doctor Octopus. *Spider-Man 3* features three villains. Osborn's son, Harry, becomes the New Goblin. Sandman is a monster who can change shapes. And Venom is created when an alien life-form combines with a human.

Spidey fights Sandman in *Spider-Man 3*.

Spidey's Struggles

In the first Spider-Man film, Peter Parker's uncle Ben tells him "with great power comes great responsibility." The character struggles with that message in the next two films. Peter Parker realizes that being Spider-Man means pushing away from the people he loves. He must protect them from villains who want to destroy Spider-Man.

❝The strength of ... Spiderman or Peter Parker has always been that he's one of us.❞
—director Sam Raimi

DID YOU KNOW?

Some studio officials were horrified when they saw the first computer-generated shots of Spider-Man. The action looked so real that they thought Tobey Maguire was actually doing the stunts!

#10

Indiana Jones
Thrills and Spills

Movie fans look for three things in their action-adventure heroes. The heroes must be able to laugh at danger, laugh at pain, and—every so often—laugh at themselves. That is the secret of Indiana Jones. Jones is the creation of two talented filmmakers, George Lucas and Steven Spielberg. Along with actor Harrison Ford, they made *Raiders of the Lost Ark* feel like a roller-coaster ride.

CHARACTER STUDY

Character: Indiana Jones
Creator: George Lucas
Movie: *Raiders of the Lost Ark*
Year: 1981
Actor: Harrison Ford

Cliff Hangers

During the 1930s and 1940s, movie theaters usually screened an episode from a film **serial** along with the main attraction. Each episode of the low-**budget**, high-excitement serials was a few minutes long. It usually ended with the hero moments away from death. It was a smart way to get people back into the theater the following week. George Lucas wanted to make an entire movie in the same style.

Lucas asked his friend Steven Spielberg to direct *Raiders of the Lost Ark*. Spielberg had directed the blockbuster *Jaws*, among other films. They chose Harrison Ford to play the lead role. He had been in two of Lucas's most successful films, *American Graffiti* and *Star Wars*. Ford could make action scenes look scary and fun at the same time. He was the perfect Indiana "Indy" Jones.

Action hero Indiana Jones is known for his bullwhip and beat-up fedora hat.

CLASSIC QUOTE

"I'm making this up as I go!"

—Indiana Jones, explaining his "plan" to steal the lost ark

Great Escapes

When *Raiders of the Lost Ark* was released, Indiana Jones instantly became one of America's favorite movie characters. The thrill-seeking college professor is searching for a golden ark that holds the Ten Commandments. Along the way, he battles everything from poisonous snakes to **Nazi** villains. He makes one breathtaking escape after another—only to find himself in trouble again a few minutes later.

In one of the film's most famous scenes, Indy comes face-to-face with his biggest fear: snakes.

Raiders of the Lost Ark was a huge success. Plans began immediately to make two more films. The films *Indiana Jones and the Temple of Doom* and *Indiana Jones and the Last Crusade* were big hits.

THE INDY FILES

The adventures of Indiana Jones are not limited to the movies. On TV, Sean Patrick Flannery played Indy in *The Young Indiana Jones Chronicles*. The program followed Indy as he traveled the world, meeting famous people and getting caught up in important historical events. Fans can play Indy in video games. They can also scream along with Indy on rides such as Disneyland's Indiana Jones Adventure: Temple of the Forbidden Eye.

An Old Friend Returns

The Last Crusade was released in 1989. Fans had to wait nearly 20 years for to see Indy on the big screen again. Finally, *Indiana Jones and the Kingdom of the Crystal Skull* arrived in 2008. The film takes place in the 1950s. The movie shows Indiana Jones as an older (but not much wiser) adventurer. This time, he must deal with Russian spies and aliens—and survive a nuclear blast!

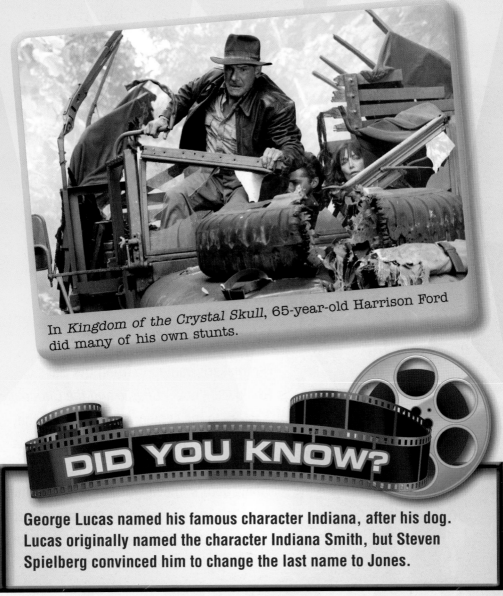

In *Kingdom of the Crystal Skull*, 65-year-old Harrison Ford did many of his own stunts.

DID YOU KNOW?

George Lucas named his famous character Indiana, after his dog. Lucas originally named the character Indiana Smith, but Steven Spielberg convinced him to change the last name to Jones.

Napoleon Dynamite

Movie: *Napoleon Dynamite*
Year: 2004
Actor: Jon Heder

Napoleon Dynamite is a clumsy, quirky teenager who is trying to survive high school. Along with his friends Pedro and Deb, his brother Kip, and his Uncle Rico, Napoleon tries to make sense of life in his small Idaho town. Together, they discover that the key to happiness is being happy with who you are. *Napoleon Dynamite* was a surprise hit. It made $44 million, more than 100 times what it cost to produce.

Willy Wonka

**Movie: *Willy Wonka &
the Chocolate Factory***
Year: 1971
Actor: Gene Wilder

Filmmakers wanted to bring the classic Roald Dahl novel *Charlie and the Chocolate Factory* to the screen. But they knew they had to find the perfect person to play the odd chocolate maker. After considering many actors, they settled on Gene Wilder. Wilder's Wonka was both strangely stern and kind, and he remains one of the most memorable movie characters ever.

Glossary

Academy Awards: awards given each year to members of the movie industry. Several people are nominated in each category. The winner receives a golden statue called an Oscar.

animatronic: having to do with a puppet that moves so that it looks alive

budget: the amount of money set aside for making a movie

computer-generated imagery (CGI): technology that involves using computers to make the animation or special visual effects for movies

dialogue: the conversation between characters in a movie

Great Depression: a devastating worldwide economic downturn that began in 1929

icon: a person who symbolizes a popular idea

Nazi: a member of a political party prominent in Germany in the 1930s and 1940s. The Nazis were known for their brutality and racism.

rights: the permission to make a story into a movie

samurai: a member of an ancient Japanese military order

screen test: a short tryout that an actor does before a camera

sequel: a movie that continues the story of an earlier movie

serial: a work that appears in parts

sidekicks: characters that are close friends or buddies

sound designer: a person who plans how a movie will use voices, noises, and other sound effects

For More Information

Books

Burr, Ty. *The Best Old Movies for Families: A Guide to Watching Together*. New York: Anchor Books, 2007.

Horn, Geoffrey M. *Movie Acting* (Making Movies). Pleasantville, NY: Gareth Stevens, 2006.

Simpson, Paul. *The Rough Guide to Kids' Movies*. London: Rough Guides, 2004.

Thomas, William David. *Johnny Depp* (Today's Superstars: Entertainment). Pleasantville, NY: Gareth Stevens, 2007.

Web Sites

Academy Awards Database
http://awardsdatabase.oscars.org
Go to this site to find out who was nominated and who won every Oscar in history.

Yahoo! Kids: Movies
http://kids.yahoo.com/movies
Watch clips and learn more about popular movies for kids.

Index

About the Author

Mark Stewart has written more than 200 nonfiction books for schools and libraries. He does not claim to be the "ultimate" movie author, but he did once star in a movie. Mark played Zachary Zween in the 1971 film *The Story of Zachary Zween*. It was based on a book of the same name by Mabel Watts. The movie was not a blockbuster, but Mark's daughters get a kick out of watching it today.